42 Days
POSTPARTUM

A New Mom's Candid Memories

Joclyn M. Polhemus

Fulton Books
Meadville, PA

Published by Fulton Books 2023

ISBN 979-8-88982-401-5 (paperback)
ISBN 979-8-88982-402-2 (digital)

Printed in the United States of America

Contents

Postpartum

The postpartum period is most defined as the first six weeks after birth (or forty-two days) associated when a woman who is not breastfeeding would typically get her first period less aligned with the time it takes to fully recover from childbirth; full recovery can even take a year.

Warning: This is a book comprised of a real first mother's candid thoughts and experiences during childbirth and the commonly defined postpartum time frame. Read at your own risk.

Introduction

It was placed on my heart during my eight-month mark to write this book. I am in no way an expert on pregnancy as this is my first; however, I have always had a passion to help others especially in the topic of health and wellness. With health and wellness comes self-care, a component we often neglect. In writing this, I am hoping that my candid transparency helps another woman along the journey. Carrying, birthing, healing, and raising children is no easy task, but our bodies are amazing and have been blessed with the mechanisms to do so.

For those who have struggled with fertility, you are strong. Don't let anyone say otherwise. It is not always easy physically, mentally, or emotionally, but know this (from a spiritual perspective): there is a purpose for everything, and timing is not determined by us alone. Though some of us may not carry, we may become parents in other capacities. From mentorship to another child, surrogacy, adoption, fostering, childcare, godparents, aunts, and more, it takes a village, and you are capable.

A Letter to My Husband

Joclyn M. Polhemus

April 11, 2021

Dear Michael,

We have chosen to embark on this journey together, and there have been wonderfully easy days, and then there have been difficult, stressful days. Regardless of what type of day it has been, I'm glad I can turn over to my left or my right and see you there, present and attentive. When I am tired, stressed to the max, you swoop in and recognize when I need time for myself. I have seen new qualities in you that I didn't see before, such as your organization skills with the linen closest. All jokes aside, I step back and look at how we are evolving in this dynamic experience. Our baby girl is so precious that she makes us want to go through the process again, and I'm so happy that I get to go through this process with you. Even though you would like us to go through this as the number of digits on your hands, I'd rather lower that number but gladly welcome us building our family. No matter what, I know we have given this all to God, and whatever is his will will be the way. I look forward to walking our designated path together and seeing how our lives unfold.

Forever your loving partner,
Wife

A Letter to My Daughter

April 11, 2022

Dear Mahalia,

I write this letter as you are sleeping swaddled in your 4moms MamaRoo. You are the most beautiful, precious, tiny human, and I am so proud to be your mother. Regardless of the stress or the pain that I have gone through, it has all been worth it. Your bright, beautiful eyes warm my heart every day, and our snuggles just make our bond even sweeter. Every moment is a favorite moment that I don't want to forget, but when we sing "Unforgettable" by Nat King Cole and Natalie Cole, my eyes swell with water because I imagine how you will grow and blossom into a beautiful, smart, creative, loving young lady.

It is my hope that you always know that I love you and that I am here for you. When you get older, there will be times where we may butt heads or you may feel that you can't tell me something, but please know I am always here, and no matter what, I will always love my baby girl. Know that you can come to me. Know that I will always love you. Know that I will always do what moms do and that's pray over you. From the day you were born, I would pray silently over you while caressing your head. When you broke out with a rash from a reaction to something I am still unsure of, again I laid my hands over you and prayed for you. When you sleep peacefully, I pray over you. When you get older, I will still pray for you. From your first time driving by yourself to going on your first trip, from your first competition to your graduations, I will continue to pray over you. From your first job to you having your first child (if you choose to), Mommy will be clasping her hands, praying over you, remembering the little head I caressed on the first day you were born.

Lastly, I would like to pass on some advice my mother always gave me: "It'll work out. It always does." I am sure this very line that my mother said to me will be said to you as well. I am thankful that I was blessed with such an honor to be your mother, and I look forward to watching you grow gracefully into the person you were always meant to be. As always, Mommy loves you.

With the love in my heart and
the prayers on my lips,
Mom

How It All Started

While I was deployed in 2021, my husband and I discussed and made the decision to start having kids or at least try when I came back. My husband was thirty-three at the time and I was twenty-seven. Boy, oh, boy, we had no clue what we were getting ourselves into, but nevertheless, we were both down for the journey.

We tried for the first time, and nothing happened. My period came as usual, and I felt somewhat sad. My husband later shared with me that it crossed his mind that maybe he couldn't have children. I never knew that such a thought crossed his mind.

Another month passed, and I got weird dreams. These dreams were vivid pregnancy dreams. I glanced at my flow tracker and realized my period was coming soon. I decided I would take a test in a few days.

At the same time, I had planned a trip with my dad, little sister, and brother to see my grandmother in Northern Virginia. Right before the trip, I took a test. Behold! It was positive. I stood there in disbelief with a rush of happiness. Then I paused. I remember speaking to myself in my inner voice, *Don't get too excited. Let's wait a few more days and take another test.*

Along the trip, I had the worst cramps and was very tired. Surprisingly, my father had no clue the entire time (or so I thought). I tried so hard not to make it obvious as I had not shared the news with my husband yet.

My aunt, however, read me like an open book. She watched my movements closely and my reaction to the cramps and looked at me in my eyes and said, "You're pregnant, aren't you?"

I stood there with a blank stare. My secret was exposed. I responded, "No one knows yet." I couldn't lie.

She told me not to worry and that she wouldn't tell anyone, then started grinning hard and told me to sit down and get comfortable. A part of me was relieved that someone knew.

Later that day, I took another test in the hotel. Lo and behold, it was positive again. I was uber excited to make it back home to tell my husband the big news.

On June 20, 2021, my husband found out that he was going to be a dad. I remember it so well. He was asleep, wrapped up like a tight burrito in the king-sized, Target knitted blanket on our platform bed, snoring comfortably like a big bear. I originally wanted to wake him up with coffee, and once he finished, the bottom of that coffee cup would say, "You're going to be a dad." Well, that didn't work out. I was too wound up with excitement to wait. I woke him up. With the mug in my hand, I asked him, "What's on the bottom of this cup? Is there something in here?" Half asleep, half awake, with eye crust in the corners, he stared at the bottom of the cup. Seconds went by as he tried to get his eyes to focus. Then, suddenly, his eyes grew big.

"What!" he exclaimed. "Are you serious? You're pregnant?" he continued.

In excitement, a few curse words were dropped, typical. Then we both teared up or at least I know I did get cloudy eyed. It felt official. It felt finally official. We were going to be parents!

We eventually told the grandparents later that same day through FaceTime. My mother-in-love was in Food Lion when we called. Bystanders would probably ask, "Why is she crying in the middle of the baking aisle?" But they were tears of joy, and we cried right along with her. My parents were sitting in the man cave. I kept calling my older sister to try to get them together and call me when they were settled. It took a while to finally get ahold of them, but once we did, my mom screamed.

The first appointment was scheduled to confirm. I was seven weeks gestation—seven weeks and experiencing cramps like never before.

The Birth Experience

It all started on February 23, 2022, at around 4:00 a.m. How did I know? Well, I woke up to pee, and when I wiped myself, blood of a pinkish hue damped the toilet paper. *Finally!* I said to myself. Something was finally happening that was showing me there was progress. What was even better was that my doctor's appointment for my weekly checkup was scheduled that day as well for 7:00 a.m. I was eager to see what my progress would be.

At my appointment, for the first time, I elected to have my cervix checked. On any of the previous checkups, I refused if nothing was going on down there. Why would I put myself through this uncomfortable experience? Yes! Uncomfortable it was. The midwife put on gloves and lined her fingers with lubricant. Due to my cervix being way back and not dropped fully, she had to reach in further. This was very painful for me. I almost squirmed off the examination table. However, requesting the exam was worth it as I was informed that I was one-centimeter dilated and 60 percent effaced. When her hand finally came out, for what felt like an unforgettable ten minutes (really, it was two minutes of that), she also confirmed I was starting the bloody show.

According to What to Expect, bloody show is "a discharge of mucus that's tinged pink or brown with blood." My experience with bloody show was a combination of mucus and streaks of blood that lined her fingers. When I saw that, I knew it was really happening. She proceeded to inform me that she wouldn't be surprised if I gave birth that day or the next two days. She was definitely positive that I would not make it to my forty-week appointment the next week.

After my appointment, I immediately texted my husband to inform him of what took place. He took off the rest of the week; he didn't want to miss a beat. I then called my mom to let her know. Her response was, "I'm on my way." This is just one part of the supportive tribe I have during this season, and you will see as you continue to read just how much of a blessing it is and what it means that it takes a village. I just thank God that my village is strong, encouraging, and supportive.

All throughout the day on the 23rd of February, I did things to help labor progress naturally. My mother and I went on walks (twice that day). I bounced on my yoga ball for ten minutes at a time several times a day. I enjoyed a wonderful seafood boil and got massages (my favorite part). During the day, I experienced contractions eight to ten minutes apart lasting about fifty seconds. These were painful unlike the Braxton-Hicks contractions that would just take your breath away. The best way to explain/describe how the contractions felt is that they would feel like a wave. Starting from my back, gradually, the pain would peek to a serious cramp in my stomach. After it would peak, the pain would slowly melt back into my back. What helped the most for the contractions was deep breathing. In fact, the deeper I breathed and exhaled with a sigh, the pain would slightly subside and was more bearable. I was so uncomfortable that sleep was not easy. I finally decided around 11:00 p.m. that I was going to try to get some sleep, especially when the contractions had seemed to stop.

Around 12:51 a.m. on February 24, 2022, the contractions kept waking me up out of my sleep. It was so painful, and I was in a zombielike state going in and out of sleep that I didn't know how far apart the contraction were exactly. I texted my mom and asked if she could lay near me to count while I tried to get some sleep. By the fourth or fifth contraction, my mother said that the contractions were real close and maybe we should head to the hospital. At that very moment, another contraction came, stronger than the other, and I responded "okay." As I started to get ready to head to the hospital, I had three to four more in just fifteen minutes with one more on the car once we parked in the hospital parking lot.

In the process of checking into labor and delivery triage at 2:20 a.m., I had another contraction trying to give the intake nurse my information. Let me start by saying that the Riverside Regional Medical Center Labor and Delivery/Postpartum staff were amazing! Even though I had some unexpected moments, they made the experience a great, caring experience.

While in triage, I was hooked to a monitor that monitored both the baby's heart rate and my contractions. They also took a pee sample, blood pressure, and temperature and did another painful cervical exam. Still in the posterior position, my cervix was two to three centimeters dilated and 60 percent effaced. After monitoring for an hour and giving me juice and water, they had concerns about the baby's heart rate because there was no deviations or reactions to stimuli, just a steady pace. It was then that the midwife asked me if I wanted to be admitted or go home. I asked to be admitted; there was no way at this moment with the contractions and fetal heart rate that I was going to volunteer to go home.

Before moving me to my next room, they set an IV. The nurse kept hitting valves. So they went to another arm and used this cool device that mapped out my veins to avoid hitting a valve. After the IV was administered, I got this sudden urge to pee. As I went to pee, I felt a warm trickle down my leg. Immediately, I thought my water broke; but to my surprise, my husband informed me that is was actually a blood clot, blackish-red in color. I got concerned and asked my nurse. She informed me that it was normal, still the bloody show. My cervix was ripening.

Around 3:30 a.m., we moved into the labor room. I shuffled through the hallways with my fluffy socks on into the room. The room was very nice and spacious. We were in the room for about two hours before I asked for an epidural as the contractions became so painful that they were unbearable and giving me the shakes. Unexpectedly, compared to the contractions, the epidural was a piece of cake. The anesthesiologist was very informative and walked me through the steps of the process. It was a nice feeling to have my husband in front of me as I went through the experience; the numbing medication was the only sensation of pain I felt. The moment the medicine entered the spine, I felt burning spreading out of the spot. When the epidural test doses were administered, I felt a weird ache in my butt but not painful. When the actual medication was administered, I felt a cold sensation enter the body. It took about twenty minutes for the medication to fully take effect. My legs felt heavy, but the top half I could move. A catheter was put in place since I would not be able to control my bladder.

At 6:30 a.m., I received my fourth cervical exam. At that moment, I was seven centimeters dilated and still had some thickness of the cervix 60 percent effaced; therefore, the decision was made that no Pitocin was going to be administered because I was progressing well on my own. However, they had me switch from side to side because the baby was on her umbilical cord, and they thought it was being compressed. They used what was called a peanut ball to elevate the compression one side at a time. I then got a delivery of fluids, which was allowed to be ingested while in labor. There was coffee, apple juice, tropical Jell-O, and chicken broth. Let me just say that chicken broth was *amazing*! Either it really was the best chicken broth ever or I was just hungry.

Eight o'clock in the morning came and went. I started to get gassy a lot. It almost felt like I pooped on myself. I had to get my mother to check down there to see if I did. At 8:37 a.m., the midwife checked me and said I was five centimeters dilated, not seven centimeters dilated, and 70 percent effaced. The baby was also very low, and that was why I felt the back pressure ache pains. At 11:25 a.m., there was no changes. My right side was cramping, but I pressed the epidural button for more medication, hoping the pain would ease. I was checked again, and it was said that my cervix was still thick. I asked myself, *If gravity helps with labor, why do they keep putting me on my sides and expect me to progress?* At this point, I was annoyed and tired with the right-sided cramps that I had trouble convincing my eyelids to stay open.

At around 2:00 p.m., I felt lots of pressure to poop. The midwife and nurse were called. Finally, I was ten centimeters dilated. However, I still had a lip of thickness for my cervix, but we could start pushing. The pushing was something I was not ready for. The midwife asked if I know how to push. I answered "no." She then instructed me to push into the area she was touching, bearing down like I was going to poop.

On the first push, I inhaled and then pushed down hard, but my hard was not hard enough. It took three practice pushes and the threat from the midwife that if I don't push, she would turn down my pain medication for me to finally get the hang of it. What felt like forever was probably twenty minutes of pushing, and her head was out. The most painful part of the birthing experience for me was when I was pushing. I could feel the tear, and the more I pushed, the more it felt like I was tearing it more. I became apprehensive. I thought I was making it worse.

The next actions were swift. The midwife carefully, skillfully, and quickly unraveled the umbilical cord from around her neck. The next push she assisted in pulling her out, and her entire body was laying on my upper stomach, covered in the fluids and layers of the gook being inside the placenta. I could have cared less; I had to touch her. What was tears from pain turned into tears of joy and astonishment. I thought to myself, *This is real.* I looked at my husband, the one who said he wouldn't cry, and tears of love fell down his face, tears I've never seen before. My mother was crying too. It was a boo-hoo fest. The eventful day didn't end there. Apparently, my cervix was lacerated, and my perennial area was torn. There was a lot of blood, or so I was told, even after the placenta was pushed out. The midwife examined my insides, and I noticed that she was perplexed. She paged for a doctor consult while packing me with gauze. My mother stayed to my right, and my husband stayed with the baby as the nurses cleaned her up and performed the necessary checks. Her original color was blue. It took five minutes for her to gain color fully, and then she was pink.

The doctor came in for the consult. My legs were still wide open and packed with gauze, and the baby was being checked in the background. The doctor tried to do something, but that something did not work. She witnessed the pain I was in. The repair that needed to be made to my cervix was extensive. She immediately put in for me to go to the OR and paged anesthesiology to give me more medicine for the procedure. The doctor continued to pack my womb with gauze to control the bleeding. In roughly ten minutes, I was rolled to the OR. The OR was bright, and drapes were placed over me. Many people were in the room, moving fast, setting up surgical instruments, prepping, scrubbing, and administering meds. I've only had surgery once, and that was on my two front baby teeth after a fall on the tile floor racing with my sister in the house. Never have I ever had surgery since. Surprisingly, I wasn't scared. The anesthesiologist pumped this medication into the epidural line, and before I knew it, I was knocked out. I remember nothing from the surgery—absolutely nothing. I like it that way. I woke up to being in the recovery room with two nurses. I also remember my husband, my baby, and the NICU nurse in the room waiting to transition with me to the postpartum department. While lying in the hospital bed, I felt nauseous; and immediately, I said, "I have to throw up." They raised my bed, and the last thing I remember was uncontrollably throwing up, and then I blacked out.

(I'll let my husband tell it from his point of view to capture the time where I was blacked out in the recovery room.)

I remember them saying, "There's the head." It's the thing that men see and go, "Oh, shit!" I remember them telling my wife to do a couple more pushes. I didn't want to look anymore. I looked at how hard my wife pushed, and a few moments later, I heard our daughter's voice for the first time. That was the moment I realized I was a dad to hear life in her voice. They were trying to clear out her nose and clean her up. The baby gave the doctors a stinky face. They placed her on my wife's chest and gave me some scissors to cut the cord. I remember that moment as a moment of joy. Simultaneously, I overheard the doctors discussing a tear. At that point, I did not know what to think. They were cleaning my wife, and the placenta fell out. It looked like the size of a steak. The doctors then said she needed to go into surgery. They cleaned up as best as they could and took her into surgery.

I went with the baby while my wife went into surgery. I had to go with the baby as she got her first shots. They placed the ointment in her eyes. The surgery probably lasted twenty minutes. We were told to wait in the post-op room, and my wife woke up out of her sleep. They were running through questions and asking how she felt as they raised the bed up. As the bed was slowly being raised, my wife started to vomit. As she started to vomit, they asked more and more questions. The frequency of questions was coming faster. Her eyes started rolling in the back of her head. Her arms went out and started flailing everywhere. The nurse would look at me and not say anything, and I would look at my wife. What felt like thirty seconds felt like forever with the thoughts that were going through my head. I felt vulnerable without anything being said. I was thinking so many things like, *Am I going to raise our daughter by myself?* Just as thirty seconds of eternity went by, she came too. They used an ammonia cap to bring her back to consciousness. She started talking as if everything was normal. The nurse said she always hated that part of the surgery. She stated she could only think about the thoughts that crossed a husband's mind. My wife came through as if nothing happened.

42 Days Postpartum

Day 1: February 24, 2022

My legs were still numb from the epidural, but the catheter was removed. We were in a smaller version of the delivery room, but the bed was more comfortable than the delivery bed. My mother was worried because what was supposed to be a thirty-minute to one-hour procedure turned into two hours. I vaguely remember, being high on drugs, waving at my family in the waiting room area as we crossed the path to postpartum section.

The first day postpartum was spent recovering. I went in and out of sleep and needed assistance every time I went to the bathroom. Shuffling bathroom trips consisted of mesh postpartum underwear, a thick extralong pad, and a ready-to-use ice pack that you snap to activate. All that was lined up to soother the area from the recent trauma. After peeing, I would have to use a perineal cleanser spray. Spraying from the front to the back, I saturated the areas; and with a squirt bottle, I used lukewarm water to rinse the cleanser off. Then half a roll of toilet paper later, I patted the area dry. Thank God for the strength of a commercial toilet! (Don't try this at home, folks.) The ice pack was first, thick pad second, and the mesh underwear last; I pulled my new favorite lingerie up. The ice pack is my absolute favorite. Ladies, this is a great relief; the coolness helps relieve any pain and swelling. As for medications, I was placed on Tylenol, Motrin (for pain management), a prenatal vitamin (of course), and Colace (stool softener). One of my fears was pooping and getting a hernia, but the stool softener was worth it as my body had to readjust with the hormone shifts, healing down south and eating differently.

Breastfeeding was also a nervous subject for me. I wondered how bad it would hurt. The first time took a few tries to properly latch. Apparently, I was latching the wrong way as I will describe later. The initial tug hurt, and she stayed for a good thirty minutes.

Besides falling in and out of sleep, breastfeeding, and frequent interruptions from vital checks for both me and baby, I was absolutely exhausted. The blood loss from the surgery and fluid buildup didn't help either.

The first night, I barely got any sleep. Frequent feedings and bathroom breaks that took fifteen minutes too long made it hard to fall back asleep. Due to the COVID-19 visitor policy at the hospital, my mother couldn't stay the night. It was just Michael and I. Michael was truly hanging in there, resting when he could but taking care of the baby outside of feedings. The night went by so fast. Before I knew it, the light burst through the blinds, and it was my baby's first morning. She would sleep two-hour stretches and wake for feeding.

By morning, I was elated for a true breakfast. Eggs, bacon, coffee, French toast, juice, and milk lined the table. I inhaled that food. I took my meds soon after and experienced another abdomen check. The nurse came in later to check my blood. Indeed, my iron was low due to the blood loss during the surgery. The midwife from delivery came in and spoke with me about my anemia and being placed on prescription iron pills and how I wasn't anemic when I first came in. So far, my only pain was when I went to the bathroom or shift positions after sitting still for a long time.

Day 2: February 24–25, 2022

I had my first shower today, actually, more like a sponge bath. I am very particular about public showers, and the fear of a public shower curtain touching my butt made me cringe all over. You would think years of being in the military and taking showers in field conditions would make that fear go away. No, it made it worst. Anyways, it felt amazing to feel refreshed after gushing life into the world—that kind of shower. Yes, I had help. Utilize your support; otherwise, it can take a while to maneuver through the process of sitting, peeing, cleaning yourself up, and rearming with cold packs, pads, and mesh underwear. I have experienced lots of blood loss but all normal after birth. It burns to pee, and periodically, I get cramps and contractions when breastfeeding.

On breastfeeding, how difficult art thou? Latching has been painful especially on the right breast. I'm not sure if I'm even giving her enough. I find myself getting frustrated with my husband. I know he is being supportive, but the constant talks and questions about breastfeeding and trying to adjust makes me feel inadequate. I know he's curious. He wants to know how it works. He wants to be a part of the process. He wants to support the breastfeeding journey. I'm just feeling like an exhausted failure not giving enough food for my child.

Baby had her first bath today. They wait to give baby a bath until they hit the twenty-four-hour mark. So, yes, your baby will still have cheesy afterbirth on them in certain spots until the sponge bath. You will love them so much you will kiss them anyways.

Day 3: February 25–26, 2022

Today is the day. The day we get discharged. I'm so excited to go home and for our baby girl to meet the rest of the family. They told us that we could be looking at a noon discharge after a few rounds take place. The baby had to be seen by two medical personnel, and she had to have her hearing test. Like flying colors, she passed. Her two other checks cleared her for discharge way before me.

I had to await my check from the doctor, lactation specialist, and my debrief from the nurse. The doctor asked about pain levels and pretty much cleared me for discharge. The lactation specialist came in to give me a few pointers, and boy, was I grateful. The entire time, I had been holding my breast wrong, which was causing the painful latching. What ended up working for me was the cross-body hold on the right breast with a U-shaped hold on the breast. For the left breast, the football hold with the taco breast hold was comfortable. It was also amazing how the amount of pillow and back support could give me for a comfortable experience. After her suggestions and putting them to practice, I felt a little more confident that I could do this. I could provide for my baby.

Later, the lactation specialist came by again to explain expressing and the benefits of expressing. Expressing from the breast helps form the milk, bringing the milk in. Expressing before feeding is best. When you express, you are practically massaging the breast with a firm grip from the back of the breast to the areole. Then you will see the colostrum slowly ease out. Colostrum itself has so many benefits for the baby. Colostrum provides antibodies and nutrients needed for the baby's first days on earth.

We were discharged at approximately 01:00 p.m. We loaded up our hospital favorites: big-ass pads, ready-to-use ice packs, and mesh underwear—all amazing. They also gave me a sitz bath kit, belly binder, tub, water jug (the right of passage for labor and delivery), perineal spray, squirt bottle, formula, diapers, wipes, baby hats, hospital swaddles, nipples, pacifiers, and more. I basically felt like we went shopping at the hospital, however, rightfully so.

On average, it costs about three thousand dollars out of pocket for childbirth; therefore, in my opinion, enjoy your hospital food, take that shopping spree, pick the nurses' brains (ask your questions), speak to the lactation specialist, take your long hot shower, use the products they give you, sleep on that bed, and watch that TV. You want to bounce on the yoga ball? Do it. You want to use the peanut ball? Get it. You want pain management? Use it. Make the visit worth the out-of-pocket expense.

I was not sure what the ultimate bill for me would look like, but it was worth it. The hospital staff at Riverside Regional Hospital were phenomenal, competent, and supportive. I had no complaints. Even with my minor complication to the OR, they made my first-time birthing experience a good one.

The discharge brief was a lot of information at once. The main highlights for the baby were to not touch the stump; it would fall off on its own in a couple of weeks or so. We were also instructed not to submerge it in water until then. A tracking sheet was given to us to keep track of how many pees, poops, and what time feedings took place to ensure baby was eating enough. We were also given the talk about SIDS. No fluffy items in the crib, no co-sleeping, use pacifiers, and let the baby sleep in the back position.

In my head, my nerves ran rapidly; more concerned with the baby, I discarded my own list of postpartum care from my memory to make room for hers.

From what I could recollect, my instructions were no lifting over eight pounds, keep the vaginal area clean using the cleanser until the bleeding stops with flushing, use nonfragrant soap in that area, drink lots of water, take medication according to the prescription, get lots of rest, don't frequent the stairs, and make sure I schedule my postpartum appointment. Saved for last was the talk of baby blues and postpartum depression. If your baby blues goes past two weeks, it could be a sign of postpartum depression. These are things we should not be ashamed of. I was trying to stay aware of my feelings to be cognizant of the way I was healing—physically, mentally, and emotionally.

On the ride home, my husband drove super slowly and tried to avoid every pothole. We alerted the family that was patiently waiting for her arrival. We got to the house, and balloons were tied to the garage door, announcing, "It's a girl." As soon as we came through the door, grandparents, godparents, and my little brother were in the foyer taking pictures in awe with smiles plastered on their faces—priceless moments. As we went upstairs, a spread graced the kitchen counter. I ate so much delicious food. It was nice to have food with a little bit more flavor. After the food, I showered with the assistance of my mother and with the help of a shower bench. That was the best shower I had had in a while. I was in bliss. Meanwhile, Mahalia was making her rounds, greeting everyone with her eyes peacefully closed. Lots of photos were taken.

Day 4: February 26–27, 2022

I was so glad to have support on our first night home. My dad, mom, and little brother stayed the night. Michael and I tried to sleep in the same room with the baby in the crib. *It did not work!* For some reason, we both consistently kept checking to make sure she was breathing in the crib, and it was hard to see. Then we slept on the trundle and daybed, me on the bed, Michael on the trundle. If you know my husband, you know that he snores—loud. During pregnancy, we either slept in the same bed with me having earplugs in or in separate rooms. With the baby in the crib on the first night, there was no way I could sleep with the earplugs in. During the first cry, I tried to stir my husband, yelling and poking him, but he wouldn't wake up. I got out of the bed, took the baby out of the crib, and proceeded downstairs to the family room. I knew my dad was still up as he was a late sleeper. It worked perfectly. Every time she needed to feed, I woke up to feed her, and then she went back to my dad for burping, sleeping, or changing. That was the only way I was going to get some sort of sleep. Around 4:00 a.m., my parents switched shifts to my mom taking on the changing, burping, and watching duties. Before I knew it, I *opened* my eyes to daylight, a crisp Sunday morning.

My husband was so tired, and so was I. You don't get much sleep in the hospital as they check on you every hour, both you and the baby and not at the same time, then you're in an unfamiliar environment with an uncomfortable bed and hit-or-miss food. When I woke up, my mother was on shift, and I finally felt a little rested and ready to start the day. That support meant so much to me. If my parents weren't there, I had no clue how Michael and I would have made it through the night without me having a breakdown.

Breastfeeding is still painful as my nipples are sore/sensitive. She easts about every two hours, and no, I don't get sleep when she naps during the day. I only get sleepy at night; it's hard to sleep during daylight. I always flinch on the initial latch because it really does hurt. My husband is all about breast-feeding, sometimes too much for my comfort. I find myself more self-conscious and embarrassed and have no clue why. I don't like it when he watches, and I don't want to be touched there. I know he's just trying to help. He reads, watches videos, and asks plenty of questions to learn more and wants to share more information with me; however, I get annoyed about the constant breastfeeding talks and watching. Everyone stares. *Stop staring!* It makes me feel rushed, like I'm not doing enough or producing enough. Like breastfeeding anxiety, with exclusive breastfeeding, it was hard to see just how much I was giving her and if she was getting enough, another cause for self-doubt and anxiety.

Babies first bath at home was a good ole sponge bath. We were instructed not to submerge the baby stomach and below in water until the umbilical stump fell off. We were so nervous of the stump, and trying not to infect it, we followed all the rules:

1. Don't touch it.
2. Don't irritate it; fold the diaper so it won't rub against it.
3. Don't wet it.
4. Let it naturally air dry out (no alcohol).

With her sponge bath, we used Aveeno Baby Calming body wash, a squirt in a tub filled with warm water. I used three different washcloths: one for the face, one for the body, and one for the tush. We got in all the nooks and crannies and then dry her with a baby towel. A new onesie was put on, and just like that, we were ready for the night routine.

Day 5: February 27–28, 2022

It's a Monday, and I'm finally able to call the pediatrician. It's recommended to schedule twenty-four hours from hospital discharge, but we were discharged on a weekend. I called in the morning and got an appointment for the afternoon. This was when I realized how long it took to get ready now while in postpartum recovery and with a newborn. We were a tad bit late, but they still accepted us. So much paperwork was filled out, and I was surprised at how much information I retained. We were finally called to the back, and the hospital paperwork was turned in. Our baby girl was evaluated, and we were able to speak to the lactation consultant. The lactation consultant visit helped me gain some confidence as she was impressed with the latching and positioning,; stating there was no need for correction. (I was one proud mama.) My husband and I asked many questions, all of which had an answer. I walked out feeling better about breastfeeding; I even breastfed while at the pediatrician office.

The next goal of the day was to the get the birth certificate request in the mail. Again, a document that had some contradictions, but it was filled out the best way I knew how with an attached check of twelve dollars so that we could receive four copies. I had needed my birth certificate so many times that there was no way I was setting her up to not have hers even if it was accidentally misplaced. Due to COVID-19, it said processing could take eight weeks; luckily, we had the birth letter and her SSN on the way.

Day 6: February 28–March 1, 2022

You know how you just wish to have a clean house. Well, with being in the hospital for three days, the inability to lift, tiredness, and taking care of a newborn, the house was a mess: boxes and gifts unopened, lots of laundry, unpacked hospital bags, dirty bathrooms, a floor that hadn't been vacuumed in three weeks, and more. Luckily, my little sister came to the rescue, and with my mom here during the morning, she took care of meals and baby while my sister and I straightened up the house. My husband was getting his shut-eye from taking the night shift, which I was, oh, so thankful for. After the house was cleaned, there was a weight lifted off my shoulders, a sudden relief; it immediately improved my mood that things were accomplished.

Day 7: March 1–2, 2022

I am proud to be a PhD student at North Central University. I made the decision at six months pregnant to pursue my PhD in project management. I was very fortunate to be granted an extension due to being hospitalized for the childbirth. I knew I could catch up if I could just have an extra week. I laid out my intentions to my professor, and he agreed giving me until March 6, 2022, to be caught up with all assignments for an opportunity of full credit. I was glad this was an option instead of claiming incomplete. At first, it was hard to regain focus; but every time little lady would sleep, I would work on my modules and papers. Feedings gave me a nice break from my head being in the books.

Looking at my discharge recovery paperwork, walking was encouraged, so today was my first time for a walk. My mother-in-love (baby girl's lola) and godmother/auntie visited today, and they joined me on the walk. My motivation was reaching the coffee shop Persnickety Crane Café, a lovely place I used to work at to learn barista skills. I ordered a seasonal, Mom ordered a dripped coffee, and sis ordered a chai, and it was a nice, heavenly day. The body wrap did wonders too, holding everything in place and while walking. I'm sure I burned a few calories. There and back was about a mile walk. My husband and baby were going to join us, but as we made our way out the garage, the stroller wheel fell off the axle. My husband forgot to put in the cotter pins. Good thing it happened while in the garage and not on the way there. Walking had been refreshing. With the weather warming up and the easy routes near my house, it was a relaxing way to get some fresh air, especially when feeling housebound. Breastfeeding can do that to you, make you feel that you have to be around twenty-four seven; however, you have to make time for yourself. Get some exercise, peace and quiet, pampering time, or maybe even time to read and enjoy a fresh cup of coffee.

By the way, baby is one week old today. Time has truly flown by. It was just yesterday that I was bearing down hard, pushing in a way I never knew, to our first skin-to-skin contact. Now I have learned so much about her, from her hungry cues to eat, what it sounds like when she poops, how she sleeps, the sounds she makes, her sharp nails, to the way she smells. She is definitely a blessing and my favorite gift. Call it baby blues, but her life flashed before my eyes, and I cried thinking about how she would grow, go to school, learn to drive, do sports or arts, have a sense of style; what she would sound like; and her baptism, birthdays, Christmases, dating, and more. It has truly hit me; I'm a mom.

Day 8: March 3–4, 2022

One week down and I am 166 lbs according to the scale that I stalked. That is eighteen pounds down from pregnancy weight. I'm shocked how much my stomach has come down, but it's still loose, and I can feel things moving inside when I shift, not to mention the phantom kicks. Phantom kicks are when you feel like the baby is still inside moving, but truly, nothing is there but the organs that are squashed and acrobatically maneuvered in your body. My stomach also jiggles when it moves. Still can't fit my pants. My hips are too wide. My breast is so big the one maternity bra I purchased from Victoria's Secret laughed at me when I selected it out of the drawer. What a joke.

I'm not complaining at all, just telling the truth. I've accepted my body changes and fully know my body won't be the same. I'll be able to get back in shape and shed the weight and fit certain clothes again, but let's be real, this body has produced a life over the course of nine months and will be producing for that life for even more months. Things won't be the same. I'm just going to accept this journey with grace.

At six months pregnant, I stopped my daily yoga practice. I wish I never did that and stayed consistent. Today, I did my first yoga practice postpartum. I did a simple ten-minute practice, but it was amazing what that ten minutes did for me. I felt more relaxed. I was able to feel a deep stretch, and I was able to practice my breath with intention. It felt amazing, like a gentle wash of warm water after a long day. As I adapt more to this new life and being a mom, I will learn how to make sure yoga is in my schedule along with my daily responsibilities.

Day 9: March 4–5, 2022

Well, I just had my first explosive hormonal argument with my husband. Last night, he got so much sleep; I barely got any. To add insult to injury, he slept a lot during the day too. I woke up angry.

When I get upset, I clean hard, taking it out on every pot, pan, mug, and counter I could find. I do these things to keep my mind busy instead of dealing with the problem or talking about it. My husband could sense it all. I didn't want to argue in front of the baby either. Long story short, we squashed the beef. The lack of sleep was getting to me. The nights needed to be the time I actually got some sleep since I failed to get sleep during the day and lacked the ability to take naps during the day.

Day 10: March 5–6, 2022

Well, this is unexpected. I feel so much pressure and a tad bit of pain. I would out it as a four on the pain scale. It feels as if the insides are putting weight on my vagina, especially the clitoral region. I even get painful cramps near my anus. When calling the nurse triage to see if this is normal especially after the surgery I had, of course, they say it is normal. To me, it's a sign to increase my Kegel exercises and strengthen my pelvic floor that's still healing. It hurts when I sneeze too.

Getting ready no longer takes just thirty minutes. I need an hour just for myself. I start with brushing my teeth, scrubbing my tongue, and gurgling mouthwash. Then I hit the shower, washing and exfoliating my face. Then I wash my body. After that, it's time for lotion and nipple cream. I'm still wearing pads both for my vaginal bleeding and breast leaks. I'm all padded up and ready for war. Then begins the face skin care and hair. After that, I get dressed with a little emotional roller coaster of what I can't wear and what's not comfortable, not to mention I have to put on my belly binder to hold things together instead of giving my organs free reign on the inside.

Pumping has made things a lot easier. It allows me to have a little gap of me time. The pump I have is not the most convenient, but it was free with insurance and gets the job done. I'm thinking of getting the hands-free wearable pump, but that thing is almost five hundred dollars. However, it would be a good investment if I'm breastfeeding for a long time and for all my children, however many God blesses me with. Pumping also gives me a break from my nipples being sore/tender from latching. The main difference though is that we must give her breaks when bottle-feeding. Burping needs to take longer as well. She has a higher potential to suck in air, so that air has to get out. Babies also have the potential to overeat when bottle-fed, so having those breaks with burping in between helps with that as well.

Day 11: March 6–7, 2022

Baby is now having some crying spells with no solution or at least I thought. We would change her, feed her, and rock her, and she would still cry. Come to find out, you give her thirty minutes to work through it and sit up, and there is a poop explosion. Her poor tummy probably hurt, but this makes for a long night. I would constantly wake up thinking she needed to feed. Nope, it's gas, just gas.

With breastfeeding can come social separation. I feel that I need to be near her for when she is hungry, and oftentimes, that means not going out. This is where the jealousy and envy comes in with my husband. He can take his time getting ready at any hour. He can go out and be out for hours without a need to rush back home. I always feel that after I feed her, the clock starts for how long I can be out. I wish I could go out at any time without having to think or be confined to the walls to the walls of my home. I know it's only temporary, and providing for my baby, that's what keeps me going.

Day 12: March 7–8, 2022

Today was the worst poop explosion thus far. It's what some call a christening. Baby just ate, and

I was burping her. Her spit ran down my cleavage, how nice, and soon, a liquid fart sound vibrated my hand with the warmth and smell of baby poo. I noticed my hand felt wet, and lo and behold, my darling pooped in and sideways of her diaper. The force pushed it out of the sides. I yelled for help from my husband so that I wouldn't smear poop everywhere. My husband was in the garage, so I made the emergency phone call for him to hear me. Soon operation "get this baby cleaned up" was amid.

Soon after, she peed on my husband's hand. It was not funny, but it was funny. She has done this quite a few times and only to him. I think he has to be quicker with the diaper to cover her up before she pees. Who knows? But on the inside, I get a good laugh.

Today my husband decided to start his workout plan, which I'm happy he is getting out there during our parental leave. This is our time to bond with our baby and reestablish routines to include getting our health in check.

Day 13: March 8–9, 2022

We are going out for the first time, just the two of us. My aunt is coming over, who I'm so thankful for to watch our little one while we get some relaxation. Pedicures! We both need them, and my husband doesn't want to, but I'm dragging him along. Don't let him fool you, he enjoys them and just wouldn't do it alone unless I'm with him. I'm so ready for that foot massage, exfoliation, and paraffin wax. I haven't had polish on my toes for months because I couldn't even reach my toes; that's going to be nice too.

It was nice for us to go out, but I felt like I was against the clock, racing to get back home. During the nail appointment, I started to not feel so well. This was a result of a combination of bad, bad choices: (1) I skipped my medication at the indicated time (postsurgery), (2) it was time to eat, and (3) I did not get a good sleep last night. All of which combined made me feel like absolute crap. I had a backache and chills, my throat felt funny, and I was fatigued. I was worried I was coming down with COVID-19, and the first thing I did besides taking my medicine was take a test. Fifteen minutes later, it was negative. It would be difficult to have COVID-19 and take care of an infant. I was trying to stay away just in case.

Today is the first real bath. No more sponge baths, and she will get lotion plus a massage. We FaceTimed the family, and what do you know, she definitely enjoyed this more than the sponge bath.

We got in every wrinkle and fold, and she came out smelling like baby scent and lavender.

Day 14: March 9–10, 2022

Today marks her two-week appointment, and baby girl is still growing and thriving. She is now six pounds and four ounces. It's exactly as I guessed she would be. Her belly button stump was a little too moist for the provider's comfort, so she cauterized it. My husband and I both heard the word cauterized and automatically thought the provider was going to burn her belly button. Come to find out, it was just a solution of sodium nitrate on the belly button that would turn the area grey and dry it up. She gained a quarter inch too. My, oh, my, how she has grown.

Today I actually thought about her whole life. It brought me to tears thinking about how she would grow. It also brought up the memory of when I was a little girl and I asked my parents, specifically, my mom, one night when I was going to bed, "Who's going to take me to college?" And I cried because that was the moment I understood the process of life and death and how the people around you might not always be there. The floodgates opened all over again. I cried thinking about being here for her, myself, and her father. I cried praying that she'd get to grow up with both grandparents for a long time and that they would get to watch her grow and see her off to college (if that was what she'd choose). I love my little princess. This is not me being sad, just going through the process of realization of the circle of life. This also might be a thing of baby blues. Who knows?

As for my healing process, I just finished my last bit of pain management subscribed medications. However, things are still strange down there. I still feel dryness, pressure, and a little bit of itching in the vaginal area. I still periodically bleed, burning through pads because I change them every time I use the bathroom. Due to the constant water drinking, I use the bathroom almost every two to three hours. Every now and then, I still do the perennial spray and warm water rinse. I still pat dry, no rubbing, so I don't irritate the area. I'm also still scared to push hard when I poop, but that coalesce works wonders in putting me at ease by softening my stool.

I did a little yoga today as well. I've been striving to do at least ten minutes at every session and not overdue it as I haven't fully been cleared from heavy activity. I do Kegel exercises to where I hold tight the vaginal muscles ten times, then do a ten-second hold. This is supposed to help strengthen the pelvic floor.

I planned for after I am cleared for my postpartum visit. The ultimate weight loss goal is 135 lbs. That is five pounds lesser than my prepregnancy weight, which was five pounds lesser than my postdeployment weight. The day before childbirth, I was 184 lbs. Currently, I am at my two weeks postpartum date, and I am 164.4 lbs, almost twenty pounds down. It's amazing to realize how much the baby, amniotic sac, and fluid weighs. I also attribute some of the weight loss to breastfeeding. At the very beginning, I could feel uterus contracting with every breastfeeding moment. Apparently, it also burns calories. Another thing that has contributed is the loss of all that fluid, from excessive bathroom visits, vaginal bleeding, and night sweats; the fluid has gone down plenty.

Speaking of breastfeeding, we hit a milestone. We are now exclusively breastfeeding. At times, when I'm tired, it is very tempting to throw in the towel and reach for formula, but I stood strong to breastfeeding only. Once you witness the benefits it has for your baby, you feel more inclined to provide; and when you have a lot of support/information and become comfortable, you feel empowered. I'm confident now that I just whip it out after a shower, with little sleep, while I'm working, while on FaceTime, whenever I'm eating, in the back seat of a parked car—you name it.

I finally got to this point as I witnessed how formula or even a pumped bottle was hard on her tummy. Constant strong hiccups, explosive poops that look uncomfortable coming from her, and gas because she sucked in more air with the bottles. Yas, with breast-feeding, there is wetter and more soiled diapers at this point, frequent feedings too, but I consider it worth it if it's helping her grow, increasing our bonding, building her immune system, and going easy on her tummy. It also makes me conscious of what I consume so that she doesn't consume anything bad.

Day 15: March 10–11, 2022

I'm concerned about baby girl's belly button even after the cauterizing. It is still moist with some redness with some discharge. I pray over her every night. I'm sure it is typical of a new mom to be worried about everything and conscious of every new mark, nook, and cranny. I called the doctor and left a voicemail, and now I'm waiting. I just want to make sure it doesn't get infected. They called back for us to come in and get it checked out tomorrow morning.

Today, I had to look up what the tingling sensation meant in my breast. Apparently, it's your milk ejection reflux that causes the pins and needles sensation or milk letdown reflux. Learning all this new information about breastfeeding is very interesting. I also learned a long while ago that as long as I'm exclusively breastfeeding, no periods! It's very weird to go over a year without a period, but I'm not at all complaining. Note that just because you don't have one doesn't mean you still can't get pregnant. You are still fertile. I wonder how long our breastfeeding journey will last.

So far, through this postpartum experience, I want to share the things that have helped me with others. I know at least five women giving birth soon. I plan on making them a postpartum basket. In the baskets, I will put in items that have helped me with recovery and may prove useful. I want to help other mothers. I want to help build a strong support system with other mothers so that we can be an encouragement to one another. We should lift one another up, not put one another down. Share trade secrets of what works for one another and help one another through our toughest moments because we are tough people.

Day 16: March 11–12, 2022

Had another jealous day of sleep with my husband. I feel he doesn't understand how I don't get as much sleep as he does or how the expectation is there for me to be an octopus. Just the other day, while I was breastfeeding, I was being asked to hand him his keys from the second floor and bring it to him to the first floor. Why? I can't humbly do all these things and stay sane, like come on. When baby hits her growth spurts, she feeds almost every hour, barely giving me thirty minutes to do anything, but dinner still has to be made, dishes have to be washed, clothes have to be cleaned, house needs to be in order, payments need to be made, and homework has to be done, and I need to eat, take my vitamins, take a bath, sleep, change diapers, get groceries, make doctor's appointments, handle urgent needs, and more. I hate asking people for help and getting attitude or huffing and puffing or even "I'll take care of it" and two business days pass, knowing I would have taken care of it right then. We talk about expectations before marriage, especially during premarital counseling. Do us all a favor and talk about it: expectations and roles when welcoming a little one.

For my single moms, doing this by yourself without a coparent, I respect you on a whole different level. I watch single mothers in recovery carrying the weight of the car seat and baby whom the doctors already say are too much to carry. If pushing out the life isn't evidence that we are strong, this has to be too. We multitask without thinking about it and tap into our hurting state without question. We don't hesitate to take care of others before ourselves.

We went back to the pediatrician today to get her belly button looked at. Indeed, it is better than yesterday. Nothing is scarier than not knowing and trying to ensure everything is okay as a first-time parent. I'd rather be safe than sorry any day, and I'm not willing to gamble on my baby's health.

What's it like to be a PhD student and first-time mom? Anyone who is a student and first-time mom, kudos to you. I'm taking one course at a time for my PhD program, and some days, I want to pull my hair out. What has made this area of my life more tolerable is planning out my time, transparency with my professors, and communicating to my support team the things I need to get done (often time, that's my husband). By letting them know what I need to get done and the sensitivity of it, they are able to support me to facilitate an environment for me to get it done. For instance, I just took a test with two chances. The first chance I bombed, my daughter's crying broke my focus. I could not get my mind right. After communicating, I took my second attempt and passed with flying colors. My mother kept my baby girl soothed and occupied so that I could have a quiet testing environment.

Health wise, I stopped taking my pain medication that were prescribed; it was only for ten days. I now only have a prenatal vitamin, Colace, and an iron supplement to take. My vagina still itches, and it's hard not to want to scratch. It can be uncomfortable at times. The pressure is still there as well, especially when I go to use the bathroom. Kegel exercises are done anytime I remember. I squeeze down there as much time as I can for ten seconds, then release, repeating five times.

Day 17: March 12–13, 2022

Getting good sleep feels like winning the lottery, but even with good sleep, the mood swings are in full swing. I'm easily agitated especially with the fact that I sweat profusely after a shower as if my shower meant nothing. Or the fact that my hormones rapid that freshening up and shirt changes, and extra applications of deodorant is a must. Body odor is on a thousand, and leaking breast adds a hint of spoiled milk to the aroma. Therefore, changing breast pads is a must. Realizing the extra care for hygiene makes me even more tired.

We had more family visits today, which was nice; a little social interaction here and there is always nice. I'm not one to socialize a lot, but I know it means a lot for my husband. In this postpartum process, I realize we all have different needs in adjustments. Yes, I'm in recovery, and the baby needs our undivided attention to be taken care of, but my partner has needs too so that he doesn't burn out. He needs his strength to be that good dad who stays with the baby throughout the night, and sometimes that means the social meter needs to be fueled or he needs to get out the house or his creative side needs his attention. Him being gone, at first, for an hour or two honestly scared me. In his mind, he thinks I don't want him to go out. In my mind, I don't want to be alone with the baby and mess up or cause her to cry. However, I am slowly warming up to it, getting comfortable with being alone and not scared.

Day 18: March 13–14, 2022

I got a good sleep last night. I am sorry, though, my husband didn't quite get more sleep. It's like we are constantly doing a trade-off; one or the other gets more sleep, never equal. On the bright side, this is temporary. They say about three months is when we get that reprieve.

Baby's stump looks a lot better. It's all dried up and grey with the stain of the cauterization. A piece of scab fell off too. Now we don't fold the front of the diaper anymore. I'm still sad the doctors said I can't give her baths every night. Apparently, I was bathing her too much, and I can't put lotion on her just yet until about two months. Why? Well, frequent baths will dry her skin, and lotion doesn't allow the remaining hormones and waste to secrete through her immature pores. So, until I can, she can only bath about twice a week due to an exposing/dirty event.

We finally tried the Mylicon. It is supposed to provide instant relief for gas. It worked and got things going. We didn't use to hear or feel her pass gas, only poop, and now we do. As for breastfeeding, I pumped today for the first time in a while. I got eighty milliliters in a ten-minute pump, close to the three ounces a baby should have at two weeks per feeding. Also, I notice she tends to sleep more in the beginning of the day. Hmmm…

Day 19: March 14–15, 2022

PURPLE cry. Well, we think we have the case of the PURPLE cry:

> Peak of crying
> Unexpected
> Resists soothing
> Pain-like face
> Long lasting
> Evening

Basically, it's unexpected fussiness. It can be draining. The constant crying can take all your energy away especially when you try so much. I changed her diaper, rocked her, bounced her while on the yoga ball, gave her a passy, undressed her to give her freedom, put her in the rocker, sung to her, played music, walked with her, and nursed her, and she still wouldn't stop crying. Can I say exhausting? As my husband is the one to frequently look up things on the Internet, he came upon PURPLE crying. We will see how these next few days will go. As a new parent, we are always seeking a way to console her or fix whatever is wrong. So it is natural to be frustrated when we feel helpless. I think the best thing to do is to give each other breaks away from the crying so that we can recharge and enter the ring again. I also see nothing wrong with asking for help when we are both tapped out.

Today was a good day. No PURPLE crying. I stayed on top of her feedings and getting more predictable about her wet diapers. I find myself obsessed with her poops because I always want to know if she's getting enough from me. When I pumped, I was able to get three ounces with combining. It's such a rewarding feeling when you see how much liquid gold you can produce.

The pain and itching down south is subsiding, and now I'm experiencing new things. I've been very antsy, wanting to do and accomplish a lot but can't organize my thoughts. I write things down but scatter off onto something different. I'm trying my best to focus. I want to take my time and accomplish one task at a time, but my mind wants to do it all and do it all now. What has helped is getting outside these walls. We went for a walk today and got some fresh air. Tomorrow looks like a fine day too, so I feel we will do the same. I may even put on some makeup just for myself.

One main thing I'm antsy about is getting back to working out. I'm not cleared yet, so walking and light yoga are what I do, as well as my Kegel exercise to strengthen my pelvic floor. My yoga practices have been ten minutes in length minimum, focusing on restoring, building my strength slowly, and practicing flexibility and my breath. I'm not a runner, but I really do want to run and lift some weights or enjoy a high-intensity workout. It would be a wonderful way to blow off some steam, get fresh air, get back in shape, and have something else to put my mind on. I also can't wait to incorporate baby into these workouts. It would be a way for me to get a good workout while she gets some positive stimulation and one-on-one time while being alert, a way to build our bond.

Speaking of building a bond, can I be transparent? Immediately, when she was born, when I felt her head come out and her placenta juice covered her body, wow, laying on mine for temperature regulation, I felt a rush of emotion, a sudden this is real, this is life. I finally get to meet the one I've been carrying for nine months and experience new things with. Even after all those feelings, I still didn't feel an immediate bond. Don't get me wrong, I loved her since day 1, but I didn't feel close or connected. It wasn't until about a week ago that I felt our immense bond. As our breastfeeding challenges have faded and I've sung, read, and prayed over her every night, I have felt so close to her and felt like I understand her better. Even when I have appointments I don't want to go for long without her, like today's eye appointment I had, I texted and called my mom I wanted to eagerly get back home just to see her.

Today, I put more thought into childcare. I'm so not a fan every time I think about it. I get worked up a bit. Any good institution costs almost a whole paycheck, which is not feasible, and a nanny is just the same. Too much news has scrolled across screens and plastered on newspapers on the mistreatment of kids in these facilities and even a nanny cam in the home. Both my husband and I work, so we need something in place. I know our families would help us out, but they are too far away, and we don't want to commit anyone to that. We'd feel bad. How do I tackle this? Do I stop working? If I do, how do we get that supplemental income? Could I work out something with my employer? Do I look for other employment to work remotely? Only time will tell. Eventually, a decision will have to be made.

Day 20: March 15–16, 2022

Routines. I was asked do I have a routine. Ha ha ha ha. Nope, I don't. I've been going with the flow. I know when work is back into the picture I will need to establish a routine. I have no clue what that will look like, but I pray it fits us all.

I had my eye exam today. I knew my eyesight was getting worse during the pregnancy; I could tell. Who squints while wearing prescription glasses? Someone who needs a stronger prescription. In two weeks, this new momma will have a new sharper set of eyes.

Day 21: March 16–17, 2022

Today, I pumped and I pumped lesser than before. I feel like my milk production is decreasing. I can't lie. I'm antsy and nervous. I want to be able to provide for her. Immediately, I started looking up ways to increase my milk supply. What I am going to try to do moving forward:

- No more formula milk
- Heating pads
- Increase fluid intake (ninety-six ounces)
- Eat more (leafy greens, vegetables, fruit)
- Lactation tea
- Lactation protein shake
- Continue taking prenatal pills

- Breast massages (milk expression)
- Lactation cookies

I'm all about trying to ensure I give her the best. I even bought a new nursing drop cloth so that I am not so self-conscious breastfeeding in public. I want to be able to provide for her on demand.

Skin-to-skin contact. Baby has had a rough couple of nights, maybe a new growth spurt. I undressed her just to her diaper and did skin-to-skin contact and fed her. She slept Sunday from 10:00 p.m. to 1:40 a.m. She was in dreamland. Cool note: babies spend most of the time in REM. The slightest sound they react to may be with a quick jolt movement as a defense mechanism.

Day 22: March 17–18, 2022

I am exhausted today, but I must be conscious to eat and increase my liquid intake. I should probably fit a nap in. On the bright side, we are officially three weeks postpartum with a three-week-old baby. I have officially lost twenty-two pounds. It's crazy how fast my stomach has deflated. I'm still a little loose, and my belly skin is dark like I got a tan from stretching and releasing. As for the pain down yonder, it has minimized tremendously, and I no longer take any medications, just taking my prenatal vitamins.

As for my mental health, getting out every now and then has helped. I try to stimulate my brain every day with school, studying, or reading. I want to tap into my creative side more. I feel like I need to paint or create something; maybe I'll the patio room. I'm doing better about cooking dinner more often too. Still no real routine and going with the flow. We will see how things go.

We cannot figure out the nights. Some days, she will settle; some days, she will not. I know she's getting enough food. We exclusively breastfed today, and she has had enough wet and soiled diapers. I think she's more alert. Maybe we need to do more stimulating instead of just feeding and sleeping. Maybe we need more tummy time, colors and shapes, reading, and walks. All I know is both my husband and I are exhausted. Hopefully, we can figure this thing out soon, not sure.

Day 23: March 18–19, 2022

We tried our first outing to a sit-down restaurant with a newborn. I felt bad for the couple who ate with us. Not only did I have to slide in and out of the booth, which was probably annoying, but we had to get our little lady settled. The moment we sat down at our table, she started crying. Of course, she wet her diaper. Not a fan of community bathrooms, but I sanitized the diaper changing station in the bathroom and then laid things out as quickly as I could as she was super fussy. It took me twice as long to change her than at home. My mind was all over the place.

Once I finished in the bathroom, we sat down, and she started crying again, a hunger cry. I told my husband to look in the diaper bag for her formula bottle. We had formula but no nipple because I forgot to pack more nipples! I was frustrated at this point and hadn't even ordered a water yet while my stomach growled from hunger. My husband sensed my frustration. Sometimes, it's hard to think when she cries. He told me to order and that he would take her outside to soothe her until I could meet him outside and nurse her. It was a late Friday afternoon nursing in the back of my car. I don't know why I'm embarrassed about nursing in public. It's like I don't care if someone sees me, but I'm uncomfortable if someone stares. Anyways, thirty minutes later, I went back inside to the food being delivered five minutes later. My husband held her through the entire meal.

This was not what I pictured for our first restaurant visit. Oh, well. With time, we will get better, right?

It's very important as a couple to still make time for each other. It is hard. You want to ensure all your baby's needs are met. You have to make time for yourself and work, and sleeping consumes your time too. A lot of us forget to still make time for our significant others. I try to make time every chance I get. Today, we went to the skate shop and got skateboards made. Even though it wasn't quite just us two, it was something made with the intentions that he could teach me how to ride as he got back to riding. My husband, the social butterfly, sometimes calls me out of the seashell I'm quite comfortable in.

Day 24: March 19–20, 2022

Today's outing was the farmer's market. The weather was amazing, and there was enough space to walk and push the stroller. Got some nice items, of course, and happened to be there on Smithfield's twentieth anniversary. Back in 2014, I used to work at that very market when I was under an internship for a local farm. I miss those days. That small outing made me feel good. Fresh air does the body good.

Some moms have received their postpartum baskets I sent them. I'm happy they are getting them. I just asked them that they spread the love when they meet another new mom. If we support one another, send kind words to one another, check on one another, share what products have worked for us, compliment one another, and pray for one another, we could do so much positive and have a great impact on all of us in motherhood.

Day 25: March 20–21, 2022

One thing I can't get used to even as a new mom is people flaking on you when they try to make plans with you. Even now, I must make plans. I plan ahead to ensure I pump and that I'm back in time for feeding again. It's disrespectful to me when people do not respect other people's time. We're all adults. If you do not feel like going out, just say so. It is hard for me to have friends because of that very concept. My friend circle is very small and left behind in Richmond, Virginia, and my college friends are dispersed further all over the country. Where I live now, I have no friends, so I work. I barely get out, do schoolwork, and come home. Now more than ever, I feel lonely. I want some other interaction besides my husband and family. I would envision myself from time to time having coffee with a mom group like the one I saw at the coffee shop the other day, little ones playing and moms sipping on chai lattes, dripped coffees, Earl Grey teas, and more. The introvert in me doesn't want to stick my neck out to meet new people and be disappointed or overly stimulated.

The girls flaking was the start of my mental breakdown today. I was looking forward to an outing where I felt like a woman, putting on normal clothes other than maternity and wearing a little makeup with a couple sprits of perfume. Brunch sounded amazing, but once they flaked, my feelings were hurt. Then for the icing on the cake, I asked my husband the night before if brunch with the girls does not happen, can we get brunch as a family? He said yes. So either way, I would at least have brunch.

Morning came. I asked my husband what time we were going for brunch because I was hungry. He said, "I thought you were going with the girls!" As if we did not have a conversation already about how the girls flaked, and I at least wanted to still get brunch. Frustrated that I was not being heard, I added that to the hurt feelings. An hour had passed as I pumped, changed baby's diaper, and burped her, and I was so hangry. I then told my husband I'd just eat here. I sadly made my food with tears swelling in my eyes, unbrushed teeth, and no shower. I felt dirty. I ate my two Eggos and three eggs with coffee, staring at my cluttered, dirty house, which added to my frustration. All this piled up, I broke, shutting down. I started cleaning. I fussed with my husband that I did not want to talk right now, but he kept pressuring me. I stormed off into the baby's room and cried even more on the daybed trundle. I asked myself, "Why do feel this way? Why am I crying? How do I release this pent-up frustration? How do I do take care of my mental health better? Is it normal to feel this way and get to this point? I don't want my baby to feel this energy, does she? How can I do better?"

Tomorrow begins the workout. I will join the 5:00 a.m. club to release my frustration in a healthy way, and from 5:00 a.m. to 8:00 a.m., I can get some things done for myself, my peace of mind.

Day 26: March 21–22, 2022

I did my first full body postpartum workout. I woke up at 7:00 a.m., moved the car forward in the driveway, and commenced my exercise. It felt amazing, breathing full breaths of fresh air, adrenaline running, doing something besides sitting on the freaking sofa, reading and doing homework. The mind is not the only thing that needs stimulation. The physical body does too. Now don't try this at home, folks, because I haven't been officially cleared to resume exercise beyond walking, but I couldn't help myself. I promise I took my time and took it easy on my body. I will be sore tomorrow morning. I know it.

My physical healing is doing well, with pressure every now and then down below. It's my mental health that's still kicking my butt. I think I finally realize why I feel the way I feel. All this time, I lived in this area away from my hometown, I never established having friends here. As I sit in this house, my only social interaction is my husband and beautiful baby girl with my best friends an hour-and-a-half away. I never paid it any mind because I worked, engaged in school, and participated in markets for my business; I was so busy I didn't pay it any mind that I have no friends here. Now as I enter into a new chapter of my life, I realize how important some human-to-human interaction is especially someone in the same stage of life as you: married, with a child, working woman, student, military, etc.

Day 27: March 22–23, 2022

We came to my hometown to give my husband a break. It has been great. My husband can get some sleep and work on his business while my parents get quality time with their grandbaby, and I can be back home. The only thing is, I still can't get consistent sleep. The baby is sleeping soundly in four-hour stretches at night, but still I find myself waking up every hour to check on her, waiting to hear a coo, for a diaper change, or for a feeding, but here I am with dark circles under my eyes with specs of red, and she is sound asleep. I guess I'm in disbelief that she is sleeping so soundly. The difference between home and here, they wrap her up nicely with the blanket, and she's content just like that. I didn't want to over-heat her, but she likes it.

I'm feeling soreness from the workout yesterday. I walk like my back hurts, but really it's my legs—my quads, specifically—but it's that good sore. It looks like there is more stretching in my future. No lifting for not quite yet, but once I get cleared, lifting will commence. Right now, the focus is on establishing a schedule of getting active again. To be honest, that workout felt so good, and I feel more in tuned with my body.

Breastfeeding has gotten a lot better. My nipples are not as sore and raw anymore. I guess over time, your nipples toughen up. I'm still pumping about three ounces of breast milk combined. Once I get to two ounces from both breasts, I plan to start storing. I will have to read up and watch a few videos because I have no clue what I'm doing honestly, but I guess that's the beauty of motherhood: you learn as you go. Every pregnancy is different. Every child is different. Everybody is different. Each experience is unique, and you can never be 100 percent perfectly prepared even if you are the planning type.

Day 28: March 23–24, 2022

I stayed an additional day at my parents and scheduled an appointment at the nail shop I love going to back at home. It was a nice, relaxing time. I'm slowly, very slowly, feeling like myself, specifically, feeling better about myself and how I look/feel. The self-confidence is coming back slowly but surely. See? I have no problem with the way my body looks or has changed, but I surely miss being able to keep my nails done, hair done, and get massages every now and then. Self-care is serious! Self-care is a must and must not be neglected. When we start to neglect our self-care, we become negative about ourselves, and other issues start to compress and build up, and we explode or turn into someone we can't even recognize.

Younger siblings can get jealous or show some strange behaviors when a new baby comes into the picture. Though this is our first, I do have a little brother. He has definitely shown behaviors of jealousy, but it's only because he is used to being *the* baby, and it can turn into a competing war zone of loud talking, screaming, cutting people off in the middle of conversations, doing something he is not supposed to do knowingly, or even ignoring authority with a splash of back talk. For this, I think it's all about how you respond, making time to give him attention and not giving attention during negative behaviors. It's a balancing act. Reactions while in the middle of a behavior needs to be handled with care, not met with a hostile response, but you also can't respond with toleration. What that looks like for each person can be different especially depending on the behavior that has taken place. The main idea is to handle with care.

Day 29: March 24–25, 2022

Finally, I made it to my hair appointment. Nothing feels better than a clean scalp, and nothing looks more fresh than a neat retwist—another opportunity for self-care and getting back into my element. When I feel good, I'm better, and I can be better for my little one. I know that she can pick up on vibes/energy, and I never want her to feel or absorb my negative energy. I'm not just a mother, though, I'm a wife too.

As for being married, we have ignored the quality time part. Sitting on the couch and falling asleep to a show with the baby does not count. Hopefully, with the purchase of the skateboards and some clear, comfortable weather in the future, we can start the skateboarding classes/bonding. There is also a new movie that came out that we should go see. Maybe next week, I will schedule a time for us to go out and do something and have that time together.

As for our sex life, there is none right now and hasn't been during the nine months of pregnancy. We tried when I was around three months pregnant, and that did not go well. I had a terrible morning sickness, and let's just say throwing up in the middle of sex is not appealing at all. Then I had no desire for it. My body did not want to have sex nor mentally was I wanting it until the last two months. However, the last two months, my husband wasn't for it. Being able to actually see my belly turned it all into reality that there was a real baby in there, he felt that sex would hurt her. It made him uncomfortable. At month 9, during week 39, I was all for it because I was told it helps induce labor. Rejected! Again! It still threw him off. Now I still have healing down there and do not foresee any action any time soon. I know for a fact, being in tuned with my body, that my body is not ready even though my mind is saying something else. I guess we will just wait! I'm happy he has been patient during this process, and I think we have both done well managing the absence.

Day 30: March 25–26, 2022

We are one month now! Yes, it says day 29, but remember, I gave birth in February. I'm so proud to be her mother and learn so much about her. Time flies when you're having fun, right? Well, the entire month is a blur. It seems impossible that it's already here. The more I think about it, the less I like it because as time flies, the close we will be to going back to work, and I will see her less. I don't want to miss her milestones. I'm thankful enough that my job has realigned itself to have a better maternity/paternity leave package; however, I'm still contemplating where I stand in life, contemplating a job where I can completely work from home or getting my business fully running where I can be my own boss, all to have more time with my little precious one. Only time will tell, and whatever is for me will be for me.

Today, I discussed with someone the stigmatism about breastfeeding. Let's make this clear right now; you are not a bad parent if you don't. The main thing is to make sure our children are fed and healthy. What should be more important than this? Why do we throw shade on whichever direction someone chooses? All I can say is do you. I personally do both. I breast-feed for the health benefits both she and I get, plus it's cost effective and natural. But I also have a can of powdered formula on display in the kitchen counter ready for mixing. I use it when I need a consistent stretch of sleep so that I can be alive, well, and alert for her. I use it when I have long appointments because my body is not quite producing enough to feed and store at the moment. Bottom line: regardless of your reasons, you do what is best for you and your family!

Day 31: March 26–27, 2022

My bond with my little one is getting stronger! In the beginning, I felt helpless, stressed, tired, and like I couldn't understand her, and my body was doing all kinds of things. Here I am healing from surgery, stiches both inside and out, night sweats, hormones in disarray, barely sleeping, a newborn whining, an exhausted husband who's just as clueless as me, a messy house, a baby who needs to be fed every two hours or more for growth spurts, lots of people calling, etc. I'm sure I missed something in this beautiful, serene description of motherhood, but what has changed now from then? Here are five things I've learned and some the hard way:

1. *Utilize your support system.* Don't be ashamed to call on, ask for, or utilize help. That's what your support system is for. You should know the talents of each person in your support system and take that information to put their strengths to use in your time of need. Some naturally do on their own. If you have an appointment, don't hesitate to call. Have that backup so you can have peace of mind that someone you trust is there to watch your little one. My mother-in-love always brings food, and it's such a blessing. After that laundry list of a day, the very last thing you can get to is cooking a proper meal. Sometimes, I barely

have time to eat, which I need to do better since I'm breastfeeding. My mother and aunt comes at least once a week, and that's a blessing too. I can go to appointments or for my school/housework and my husband can rest or work on his business knowing someone we trust is taking care of our little girl. Our mom's mom (husband's grandma) gives us encouraging words, wisdom, and laughter when needed. On days that are most stressful, her phone call can lift your heart, and that support is a blessing too. Support comes in many different forms; it's not selfish to tap into it.

2. *Communicate.* Communication is key, whether it's with your support system or significant other, coparent, family, or employer. Be clear on what you need when you need it. I had to contact my employer to make sure my PPL was processed and correct and that a clear, concise e-mail to ensure no disruption in pay, and I received a clear/concise response from my boss and the personalist that gave me peace of mind. Communication with my husband has been important too.

My emotions have been up and down, and when I haven't done something for myself like having to wait to shower or brush my teeth because I was overwhelmed and felt that I couldn't be a foot away from our baby, I must communicate that. By understanding my mental state, he is able to support me in the way that he can. "Good communication is the bridge between confusion and clarity" (Nat Turner).

3. *Bonding takes time.* Bonding is a process. Some may bond as soon as the baby enters the world. Some may take time. I cried the moment she came out into the world because it finally felt real, a new reality, but I didn't automatically bond. In the beginning, I had thoughts that I was failing her as a mom because I thought I wasn't producing enough milk or soothing her cries or figuring out what comforts her. All these things take time. And even as the baby grows, these things change. Once I started taking better care of myself by taking some time for myself, our bond got a little better. You see, I was well-rested and felt con-

fident, and my mind was clear. I wasn't forgetting things anymore because I was exercising my body, mind, and spirit. How can you take care of someone if you cannot take care of yourself?

4. *Advice is all dandy, but experience it for yourself.* I'm writing this to support other mothers to show we are not alone. We do experience something that maybe uncomfortable for some to explain, and who knows? Some may take it as advice. However, please note everyone is different. No pregnancy is the same. No baby is the same. No woman is the same. No postpartum experience is the same. That's why I say advice is fine and dandy, but you must experience it for yourself. People are quick to tell you what you should or shouldn't do as a mom with yourself or your baby. They love to impede lots of advice because of their individual experiences. But their experience is not yours. Yours is yours alone. Don't get me wrong, some people have very solid advice, tips, and tricks, and it's completely up to you what you want to adopt, and you

shouldn't feel ashamed to let it go through one ear and out the other if you don't adopt it. Some advice is contradictory and some outdated, like drinking coffee while pregnant. My mom looked at me funny as I sipped my coffee, explaining to me how I shouldn't have caffeine. When she was pregnant, it was frowned upon. Now in the year of 2022, according to marchofdimes. org and my physician, two hundred milligrams a day is okay. What to Expect When Expecting is in accordance with March of Dimes and my physician. Bottom line: as time changes, advice changes too.

5. *Self-care, self-care, and, dammit, self-care.* As I mentioned before, I neglected the self and had a couple mental breakdowns in the process. When you feel your best, you can do your best. Sandra Oh said it best, "Self-care doesn't necessarily mean jogging." Although it could be a part of your self-care regimen, there are other things that need tending too. If you need silence, take you quiet time, go for a walk, read in a library, take a long shower. Failing to eat a proper meal? Go to

the store and pick out the healthy ingredi-
ents that you planned with intention, play
some music in the background as you cook,
and post that work of art before you devour
it. Got a lot on your mind? Write. Feel stiff?
Stretch. Need some fresh air? Tend to your
garden. Need some spiritual fuel? Meditate
or go to your prayer closet. It's not selfish to
care for and love yourself.

Day 32: March 27–28, 2022

A day full of visits, which was quite refreshing. Mother-in-love and father-in-love came by. It's
always nice and warming to see grandparents interact
with their little ones. We did a quick run to the store
as well with them, and the little one did well, but
my mind didn't. I have always been a lister, writing
and keeping lists to stay organized and remember.
Now more than ever, my mind has been slipping a
lot. I really can't think when she cries in the store,
and I just knew I got everything. When I got home,
I exclaimed, "I forgot the damn Keurig filter holder!"
This has been happening a lot lately. Just the other
day, I had my hair appointment scheduled and my

COVID-19 shot appointment. I was so excited for my hair appointment that I forgot my COVID-19 shot appointment at 3:30 p.m. later that day. Silly me! Why is my memory slipping!

Day 33: March 28–29, 2022

Today was so hard for me both mentally and emotionally. I think I'm experiencing postpartum depression. I find myself crying while holding my daughter in the middle of the night for an hour as my reheated chicken got cold yet again. I don't have thoughts of hurting anyone or myself, but I'm just sad, and as I saw my daughter look into my eyes as mine swelled with tears, I knew this was not healthy.

This makes me beg the question, Why is postpartum visits scheduled six weeks out? Why is there no check-in process? It takes a support system for sure to help keep an eye out for signs. My mother could pick up on the fact I was crying, and my husband was trying to get to the bottom of what was wrong, and my little sister called to check on me after my mother explained she was worried.

What is wrong with me? I could come from a spiritual perspective and say I'm fearfully and wonderfully made, which is true, and I do believe that.

However, my state of mind is not on the same sheet of music. I look at our baby girl, and I want to be the best for her, protect her, and love her. I want to be a good wife too. I also want to be a good person. Some things are just becoming overwhelming. How do I manage it all? How do I keep a house clean? Stay on top of schoolwork? Go back to work and be a badass? Protect my child in childcare? Continue to operate my business? Am I stretching myself to thin? Do I have to let something go? Will that truly make me feel better or is it just chemical imbalance? Is this what is throwing me into anxiety and unable to think, remember, and reason on a clear, consistent basis? I have no answers. All I know is that I'm going to find some and from a neutral party. Though I have my support system, I need to do this on my own accord without judgment.

Day 34: March 29–30, 2022

Today is my baby's one month appointment, which also makes one month postpartum. She's a whapping seven pounds and fifteen ounces. I was close to right in saying eight pounds. Last time, I was right on the money. I love that she's growing, symbolizing she is healthy and eating well, but I'm also kind of sad. Time seems to fly by so fast like a time-lapse video. I feel like I'm in a time-lapse. I wake up just for it to be 5:00 p.m., and before I know it, I'm eating dinner, and then, just a hop, skip, and a jump later, it's time to prep for bed. We sort of have a routine now, but that routine is built for when no one has to work. Soon, we will have to readjust yet again for as working parents of the traditional nine-to-five world. Hopefully, one day, we get to a point to make our own schedules.

How is it one month postpartum? I'm still healing. I know everything is not quite right. In fact, I will have to ask my ob-gyn why I have a lump on the vulva area. It wasn't there before. One thing that I'm trying to come to grasp with is the increased body odor. No deodorant seems to work. So far, I have tried reapplying and two showers a day. The discharge, sweating, and musk drive me bonkers and have me self-conscious all the time. I must figure something out.

Back to work, I thought have included how I store breast milk. Right now, I'm not producing enough. The pediatrician, also a mother, advised pumping after breastfeeding to increase milk supply and start storing, which can also help. With getting sleep during the night without the use of formula, breastfeeding and pumping can be so exhausting. I'm truly considering the mobile breast pump that fits in your bra. The free pump through the insurance is still a hassle that can be quite a fluster in the middle of the night.

Constipation is real. I feel like a clogged toilet. It has been three days since a good poop. I'm back on Colace and taking fiber powder while also eating veggies and drinking water. I have plenty of gas, though; no need for help in that department. Hoping to be regular real soon.

Day 35: March 30–31, 2022

When God tells you to move, you move. Many people won't understand, and it doesn't matter if they do or don't. It's our journey. It's my husband's journey. Anyone may say, "Don't make life-changing decisions right after having a baby." But again, when he says move, you move. So for the naysayers, I could care less. Today, my husband quit his job.

In the old-school way of thinking, a stable nine-to-five is the only way you can provide for your family, well, not in our household. How stable can a job be if they cannot even pay you on time correctly? That's not stability. How stable is a job if you come home upset and feel underappreciated? Not stable at all. My husband has always been creative and has always had the dream of his own business. He has been speaking life into it for years now. God has been showing sign after sign that it was time to move on. As his wife, I know he needed to hear that I support, understand, and am okay with the move. We will be fine. God always provides. Even in this season where we may feel unsteady at times, it is making way and room for what is to come. I'm excited for the future.

During postpartum, you may just get constipated. I have now upped my fiber intake. Benefiber, Colace, and leafy, green vegetables with lots of water are now my new best friend. It feels terrible to continue eating and not have a bowel movement. After one day of doing the exact things, I'll just say I had a wonderful visit to the toilet. I call that winning!

Day 36: March 31–April 1, 2022

The vaginal odor situation was really bothering me. I chose to start using the perineal wash again, same kind from the hospital with the warm water from the squirt bottle. I noticed a difference. Everything has not retracted back to size, and you don't want soap to get into places it shouldn't be, causing irritation or infection. I've always been curious about yoni steam, but I don't think that's a good idea until my postpartum appointment. I'm very nervous for this appointment. I'm scared that things will hurt during the exam. I'm still very sensitive down there, and I feel dry at times. Did I mention the lump I found down there? Not sure what it is, but I know it wasn't down there before. I just need to pray and not worry. Worrying gets you nowhere; it only breeds anxiety and wasted energy.

Day 37: April 1–April 2, 2022

It's day 37, and it's a great day to be alive. My energy is back up. I can do a lot more activities around the house. I have gotten over the "everything has to be done right now" attitude as the baby comes first. The mindset has shifted to "the laundry will get done," "the paper will be written," and "the car will get washed," not "I have to do laundry now or else." I will get to it in time. Time is a blessing. Moments with our daughter as she grows and changes before our eyes, these moments we can't get back. So, yes, laundry can wait!

Today, I'll finish my last paper for my second PhD course. As a new PhD student and momma, it hasn't been bad at all. Taking one class at a time and clearly communicating with my professor and advisor has been key, as well as tapping into my support system. It has been quite amazing.

Day 38: April 2–3, 2022

Sometimes, I feel that I got this; and sometimes, I feel that I don't get this. I'm all over the place at times and feel that I should be an octopus to have multiple appendages to get things done. I find myself evaluating where I stand now. Should I let something go? What is no longer serving me or my needs? Should I be stretching myself for this? And for what? What is my why?

I'm using my yoga practice and meditation to tune in, to pay attention, and to set intentions. I do not want to overexhaust myself on what is not for me, but I don't want to cut short in the midst of something I'm growing into. With prayer, only time will tell, and I shouldn't worry. I should just walk.

I posted on my Instagram to "be comfortable with the uncomfortable." Sometimes, in our most uncomfortable moments, a beautiful change blossom. Change is good; I just must accept it.

Day 39: April 3–4, 2022

Baby girl stayed with me all night. She slept six hours, woke up at 3:00 a.m., and went back to sleep for four more hours. I think we are getting closer to sleeping through the night. How come that's the first question that comes to people's mind when they see a baby? Every time my husband and I are out or on the phone with someone, the first question is, Is she sleeping through the night yet? I kid you not, the question was asked just two weeks in now we sound like a broken record constantly repeating the response that's always the same: "She sleeps three- to four-hour stretches," and then the comment "You will never sleep the same" is said. Thanks for your optimism.

Here is a list of other things people say that they probably shouldn't if they took the time to think before speaking:

- Does she keep up you all night?
- You're getting smaller.
- Does breastfeeding hurt?
- How come you use formula?
- How does it feel to be new parents?

Many people invoke their own opinions too. It can be overwhelming. As I've said before, you know what's best for you and your family only, and no one can tell you what that looks like because it is completely subjective. Some opinions that have been pressed on me lately:

- You should do the childcare with the cameras.
- We always used Huggies; you should too.
- You should try to get off formula.
- Clogged tear ducts? Put breast milk in the eye, so on and so on.

The list grows.

You try not to be bothered by the opinions and comments, but there is already some self-doubt that resonates within while being overwhelmed. The last thing a mom needs is everyone's opinion. If she needs tips or has questions, she will ask. Don't give advice where it's not needed. Hold the opinions.

Epic fail! We have been so busy, tired, and trying to adapt to changes that we forgot. My sister came over and mentioned, "Isn't you guy's anniversary coming up?" Here it is April 3, and our anniversary is two days away, April 5, and I completely forgot.

I said, "I guarantee my husband forgot too."

Indeed, he did. The shock on his face when I called and mentioned it to him was priceless.

We both truly and genuinely forgot. Immediately, I became sad. How? How did I forget and what do we do now? I came to Richmond so that he could work on his business, and we can't do nothing big or stuff that costs a lot of money because my husband recently quit his job under a mutual decision. Last year, we missed it because of my deployment. No, we are here, anniversary forgotten.

Day 40: April 4–5, 2022

Today, we decided due to our recent revelation of forgetfulness. On even years, my husband will plan our anniversary celebration, and on odd years, I will plan. It will probably help to set a reminder a month ahead to remember. I am still baffled and quite saddened that I forgot.

As I sit here and read *I Love You More Than Coffee: Essays on Parenthood* by Melissa Face, I have an aha moment after aha moment. Though each mother's journey is different, there are similarities in what we experience, especially emotionally; we may all go through a self-doubt stage where we feel incapable of being able to accomplish things like keeping the house clean, taking care of the baby, and ensuring dinner is ready while making sure we clean our own ass. In her essay, "Time to Play," her coworker gave an advice to "let the dishes pile up." When I read that, I stopped to evaluate myself. Why I overly concern myself with the domestic matters when I need to enjoy every moment that I have with my lovely baby girl. She is more important than the dishes. She comes before the dishes. I'll get to it; I don't have to stress about it. In due time, it will get done. I shouldn't allow the house's state to alter my mood; instead, I should be happy and enjoy the blessings of everything being in its place, my family in its home.

Day 41: April 5–6, 2022

Last night, I had a very emotional night. Again, I found myself crying with my daughter hearing me criticizing myself and contemplating life. Nothing in the sense of self harm but isn't it still self-harm to put yourself through the ringer? Is this truly hormones or feeling overwhelmed? Forgetting my anniversary, I say, was the tipping point. All the things I piled up included forgetting the things I've scheduled and a three-year-old screaming while a baby is crying, the challenges of the body odor, my business being stagnant no matter how much I pour into it, the stiches that I thought were dissolvable falling out, and the pain located at the lower left portion of my back as if muscles are loose.

We're almost halfway through the postpartum leave my job authorizes. I honestly don't understand how families in the past have done it on just four to six weeks of leave. They are strong and have sacrificed, but to me, it's plain robbery. This time has truly been a time of healing, adjusting, and bonding. Like I said before, bonding was not automatic. It came over time. Now I look at my daughter and see myself, and then I look deeper into those big light brown eyes and see her innocence, true beauty, and how much of a miracle she is. It's no vacation, but it's a gift!

Day 42: April 6–7, 2022

I have a laundry list for the doctor tomorrow. For the past four days, I've wiped myself, and stiches are on the toilet paper. I'm a bit perplexed because I thought they were supposed to be dissolvable. The twinge of pain is still there with certain movements on the lower left side of my back. The vaginal odor is still not under control. I forget things often. I'm taking all vitamins to stay regular. I have terrible gas that could out a crowd to sleep. Most of all, I still have these episodes of feeling down with crying spells that are more intense than when I was pregnant. Hopefully, I don't get brushed aside and my questions truly get their answers. If cleared to run, I will start running. Unusually, I crave it.

I'm sitting in the cafe writing my doctor's visit laundry list. Today is a self-care day. I'm starting my day with breakfast at the cafe, journaling and reading. Then I'm debating to get a massage. After that, I will focus on household tasks like groceries, cleaning, and laundry. Today, I had to make me first because yet again, I was neglecting things where I would be lucky to get a good shower in but still felt rushed.

Today, I decided to do a puzzle. I poured all the pieces on the table, all three hundred pieces, turned them upright, and stared at them. This puzzle resembles my life, pieces just everywhere, no organization, different shapes and sizes, and I'm slowly trying to put the pieces together. Some don't quite fit right, and I get frustrated in the process. I try to make some fit, but that's not its designated spot. Each piece has a place, but I'm not provided that information, just like life. It's not my job to know where every piece will fit, but I come to know over time. The only one who knows is all-knowing, and that is not me, but when it comes to being stuck on finding the next piece, that's how I feel stuck. I began to cry throughout this puzzle. Why is life so complicated? Because we make it so? Why am I so emotional? Why am I scattered like this puzzle?

As my husband walks over and takes the baby out of my hands, seeing my crying, tired, frustrated face, he sits next to me and begins helping me with the puzzle. That's what partners are for! In fact, I said, "Let's stop and go to bed."

He said, "No, you're almost done. Let's finish."

Completing that puzzle gave a sense of accomplishment, and being able to do it with my partner made it even better (quality time).

Day 43: April 7–8, 2022 (twenty-four hours after postpartum period)

Today was the day for my doctor's appointment. I was so nervous. I prayed I didn't tense up and that it was not as invasive as I am thought. I didn't wait long before I was called to the back. I got weighed and weighed in at 164.8 lbs.

As I walked to the back exam room, I grew anxious. The nurse made it better though. She was in a good mood and projected it. We laughed, sang the song on the intercom, and shared some real moments about motherhood. She mentioned how her daughter wanted a little brother or sister and stated how she wasn't ready for going through the process again. I asked her, "Have you tried getting her a pet, maybe a dog?"

She stated, "We tried that, and he died."

In the back of my head, I was thinking, *A dog is not like a fish where its common to overfeed, put them in the wrong water, or stress them out and go belly up. How did you manage to kill a dog?* Jokingly, I said, "Maybe she should just have her own garden. Something she can take care of that's alive but also don't have to worry if it accidentally dies."

Anyways, we moved on to the postpartum questionnaire, which the ratings were confusing. All I remember is my total score was 11. I was then asked to get undressed waist down, and they placed a cover over me. I waited for about five minutes, and the midwife entered the room. I brought up the pain on the left side of my back, the menstrual cramps but no bleeding, the body odor, and the stiches coming out when I wipe. The left back pain, she said, "We will monitor." The menstrual cramps, she said, were normal and due to the fact I'm bottle-feeding and breastfeeding, then I could be getting my menstrual cycle back. The body odor, she said, was normal and just a part of the package of hormones regulating themselves back to normal. As for the stiches, she did an examination: no sign of infection, tissue healed up nicely, and the outer stiches were just ready to come out. She grabbed the last two stiches that were there that could possibly cause infection out. After my checklist was completed, she had one of her own.

First, she asked about a contraceptive.

I stated, "We don't use anything."

She wanted me to caution that if the desire is to not get pregnant with a new baby already here, we should use some type of contraception with the pull-out method not being the number 1 choice.

I told her, "I'm still healing and sensitive down there. We are not active, but I will bear that in mind."

She proceeded to asking me when my last Pap smear was. I informed her that it's been a while; in fact, I can't remember. She asked if would I like to get it done today. Um…I responded politely but strongly, "If I won't let my husband down there, why would you think I would let you?"

She chuckled and said, "It's okay, you can say no."

I swiftly responded with "*no.*"

She then wanted me to get it scheduled for two to three months from now. Last on her list was my postpartum screening questionnaire. As a result of my slightly high score, she recommended a list of therapist on a printout. She also recommended ten minutes minimum every day of intentional fresh air, such as a walk, but I must get dressed for the day first. Noted. Challenge accepted.

That long list of therapist? Not helpful. Either they're not accepting new patients, won't answer their phones, or have below two stars on reviews. I know I should get some type of therapy, but this doesn't seem promising.

Candid Interviews with First-Time Moms

After writing about my experience, I interviewed several first-time moms about their postpartum experience. Below are their responses:

Mom 1 (Age: 29)

1. What were your fears, if there were any, as a first-time mom?

   Everything. The worst fear was being afraid my child might die from choking, suffocating, dropping him, and putting his diaper on too tight being afraid that I was going to hurt him. I was afraid he was too cold or too hot.

2. What are some things that you didn't know that you learned during your postpartum experience?

    How diapers are supposed to fit. We experienced a lot of blowouts and realized that. Breastfeeding, learning how to latch, being taught and doing it are two different things. I was often told in the hospital to use a nipple shield; I didn't feel that the hospital, such as lactations, were not helpful. I learned a lot about nursing as I go. I didn't realize how long it would take for my stomach to go down. No one told be about the wrapping and binding.

3. What was the most difficult part of your postpartum experience?

    Communicating to my partner. I'm not sure what happened. Before our child, we were able to anticipate each other's needs; but afterward, I now must explicitly ask, which added to my anxiety because I didn't want to feel like I'm telling my partner what to do. Also, me being a planner, it was hard adjusting to someone else running my life, being on my child's schedule.

4. Who were your biggest supporters during your experience?

    My biggest supporters were my sister and doulas. They were the go-tos for all the random questions and daily support of "You got this, momma."

5. What came to you naturally as you went through the postpartum experience?

    Connection on an emotional level and understanding his needs was instantaneous with my baby.

6. What's the worst advice or statement made by someone to you during postpartum?

    Breastfeeding. I'm the mom who does not feel compelled to cover up. It was 95° outside at my nephew's football game and my baby started to cry, so I knew he was hungry, I lifted my shirt up; my mother-in-law asked if I wanted a cover. I stated I did not want the cover. I was told I was being disrespectful and needed to cover up. I also experienced a lot of invalidation. I also don't like it when people talk to my son as if I'm not doing something, for instance, "Your mommy doesn't know that your feet are cold."

7. If you were speaking to a first-time mom, what would be one piece of advice you would share?

    Honestly, trust your instincts. Take your time. You know what you are doing. We put undue pressure on ourselves, and you are learning about a new human. You are doing the best you can. Ask for help when you need it. Don't be afraid to look for other ways to do things if something is not working out for you.

Mom 2 (Age: 28)

1. What were your fears, if there were any, as a first-time mom?

Paralyzed at the possibility of having PPD. It still follows me today. I have always been scared of getting intrusive thoughts. I was really scared of the mental health part of it; it was intimidating. I also had that fear in the back of my head that my partner would crumble and bail out.

2. What are some things that you didn't know that you learned during your postpartum experience?

    Stool softeners are nonsense. They did nothing for me. Prune juice all the way. I really focused on teaching myself on baby sleep and how it can vary. I didn't know how similar emotional and sleeping needs are related to adults. Adults seek others in emotional distress, and babies do the same thing. I'm a huge advocate for coregulation. This applies to so many challenges you can face like feeding, sleeping, toddler age, etc.

3. What was the most difficult part of your postpartum experience?

Physical recovery. I would do labor and delivery many times over the recovery. I had a second-degree tear, and I hadn't fully recovered from that for three months. I couldn't sit up straight for the first six weeks.

4. Who were your biggest supporters during your experience?

    In different capacities, physically, my partner was my biggest supporter. He literally held my hand while I took my first couple postpartum poops. Emotionally, my dad, first forty-eight hours I had an intense hormonal letdown, my dad was the one helping me pull back into reality.

5. What came to you naturally as you went through the postpartum experience?

    The maternal protective instinct kicked in immediately.

6. What's the worst advice or statement made by someone to you during postpartum?

Sleep when the baby sleeps. Just let him cry himself out: self-soothe.

7. If you were speaking to a first-time mom, what would be one piece of advice you would share?

    Throw away your expectations. There are so many unknowns that it's unreasonable to plan. You set yourself up for emotional challenges if you do that. Every experience is different. You only must get through that day and reset. Let go of the comparisons. Make calm and relaxation the goal rather than sleep.

Mom 3 (Age: 27)

1. What were your fears, if there were any, as a first-time mom?

    I was eighteen, had no cash, career, car, etc. So the fear of growing up all together and being responsible for a little human life was definitely scary.

2. What are some things that you didn't know that you learned during your postpartum experience?

    How real PPD is and how it can affect your for years after birth and also how important a healthy support system is.

3. What was the most difficult part of your postpartum experience?

    Relearning my body, accepting my body, mentally healing, and being away from family and at home a lot with no car while hubby was at work.

4. Who were your biggest supporters during your experience?

    My husband, best friend, and parents/in-laws.

5. What came to you naturally as you went through the postpartum experience?

Caring for my son and all of his needs. Being attentive, careful, cautious, and aware.

6. What's the worst advice or statement made by someone to you during postpartum?

    Saying "You'll be okay" after me venting about not being okay.

7. If you were speaking to a first-time mom, what would be one piece of advice you would share?

    Trust yourself; trust your body. The second you lay eyes on your little one, you'll know just what to do. Be patient with healing both physically and mentally. Be kind to yourself and have fun.

Mom 4 (Age: 28)

1. What were your fears, if there were any, as a first-time mom?

Whew, I think my first and biggest fear was my daughter not having both parents in her life and the effects that would come from that. With the youth I work with daily, I see how the absence of either parent can negatively impact a child's life. I didn't want that for her. I went into my pregnancy not only a first-time mom but a single mother as well. So how I would financially provide for her was also a fear. I bought a house while pregnant and thought, *OMG, am I going to be able to juggle everything a baby needs on top of house stuff (mortgage, electric, water, etc.), car, and the normal bills?* Her dad was not around during the pregnancy, but since birth, he's been in her life and helps financially.

2. What are some things that you didn't know that you learned during your postpartum experience?

All the things after having a child: the bleeding, the pressing on the stomach/uterus by the nurses. *Swelling!* I left the hospital and was swollen for a week and a half. I just knew I was going to pop. My daughter had a tongue-tie, which ultimately effected breastfeeding. I did so much research on that and talked with a lactation specialist, and we ended up clipping her tongue. I think breastfeeding was a constant learning experience for me. After clipping the tongue-tie, we had to relearn how to latch, and then it was learning how to navigate pumping and being comfortable nursing when and wherever. Once back at work, I had to figure out how to keep my supply up and how much am I really feeding her to make bottles for day care. How to take care of myself when sick because you can't take half the medication out there while breastfeeding.

3. What was the most difficult part of your postpartum experience?

Stabilizing my mental health. A lot had happened/changed, I'd say, right before having my daughter and within the first three months postpartum. Her dad decided he wanted to be involved. He lost his job, which meant not only could he not help financially but would have to move and not be near his daughter. I went back to the fear stated just earlier of her dad not being present in her life and what life for her would look like. If he goes to another state, is he just going to give up on a relationship with her? My mental health was just not stable at all, juggling those worries. My doula connected me to a Black therapist, and she helped me with navigating my emotions around him leaving, what being a present father would look like with him moving to Texas, and how to communicate as we start this coparenting thing.

4. Who were your biggest supporters during your experience?

Hands down, my parents. I ended up moving in with my parents once I had her and allowed my brother to cover, looking over my house. Being home and with my parents helped when it came to getting sleep and dealing with the switching hours. His mother came up and was extremely helpful when I had to go back to work.

5. What came to you naturally as you went through the postpartum experience?

I hate to sound cheesy, but seriously, being a mom came so naturally. A mother's job is to nurture, care, and love on their child, and I did just that, still doing that. I think patience for my own child also just felt natural. I would always admit that I have no patience, but her crying and the late-at-night feeding and waking up, I did not mind.

6. What's the worst advice or statement made by someone to you during postpartum?

I think my daughter had colic, so she was always upset. I had soooo many people mentioned her being hungry and "maybe you aren't feeding her enough (breastfeeding) that's why she is hungry" or "maybe you should get some formula." I am almost positive that is the last thing a mother wants to hear when she is trying her hardest to nurse her child. But when going to the doctor, they praise you for doing a good job and say the baby is at a healthy weight.

7. If you were speaking to a first-time mom, what would be one piece of advice you would share?

    Give yourself grace, girl! Motherhood is not easy. Appreciate the time you get with your baby and as you guys teach each other.

Mom 5 (Age: N/A)

1. What were your fears, if there were any, as a first-time mom?

    I had so many fears. I was nervous about childbirth, anxious to meet her, and fearful that I wouldn't be able to give her everything she deserved. I was fearful of all the unknowns—being someone's mom and not having all the answers. Babies truly don't come with instructions. LOL.

2. What are some things that you didn't know that you learned during your postpartum experience?

I learned so much about myself. I learned that all the hormones I had throughout pregnancy wouldn't/didn't just go away—and those caused so many different emotions that were hard to explain for the first few weeks after birth. I knew babies were hard, but there aren't enough newborn preparedness classes or books that could have prepared us for all the curveballs our daughter threw us. She's definitely proof that every baby is different.

3. What was the most difficult part of your postpartum experience?

The most difficult part had to be the physical healing and the roller coaster of emotions I experienced the few weeks after birth. We were induced, and while that process went smoothly, the entire process after she was born was super scary and showed us how serious birth could be. The healing from that physically and mentally took a while, and all this was on top of the roller coaster of emotions—being so overwhelmingly happy to meet your new little one mixed in with random bouts of crying because you don't "feel like yourself."

4. Who were your biggest supporters during your experience?

I can't say enough how amazing my husband was during the IVF process, pregnancy, and birth. He was and is my absolute biggest supporter and advocate when I needed it, but that's no surprise. Both of our families are and were instrumental as well—my mom still helps out extensively even today and is there whenever we need another set of hands or even a break. Our families have always been there if we needed anything and have all continued to show us love during this entire time. That all makes a huge difference.

5. What came to you naturally as you went through the postpartum experience?

Loving my daughter. I was nervous I wouldn't know what to do before she was born, but as soon as she came into the world and the initial few seconds of shock wore off, I jumped into mommy mode immediately. My instincts with her shock me even today—but they definitely kicked in much faster than I ever knew possible. My daughter is literally the first diaper I've ever changed, so my experience with babies was minimal to none—I was very shocked with how natural I felt and feel with her.

6. What's the worst advice or statement made by someone to you during postpartum?

    I didn't really get any negative advice postpartum. But I have gotten a ton of advice that either didn't apply to us or simply sounded wrong while I was pregnant. My advice to any new mom is to please take unsolicited advice with a grain of salt, and if it sounds wrong, it probably is.

7. If you were speaking to a first-time mom, what would be one piece of advice you would share?

If I were speaking to a first-time mom, I'd tell her what my sister-in-law told me, "Give yourself grace." That's the single piece of information I feel any new mom, especially a first-time mom, can use. You're new to this, and so is your baby. Both of you are learning and growing—together. There's no one way to parent, and you have to find what works for your baby and family. I'd tell a new mom it's fine to take advice, but it's also fine to stand up for what you feel is right for your child. You're that child's mother, and ultimately, you know what's best. You've got this! Welcome to the mommy club!

Fast Forward

Reflection

As I sit back and reflect, I am now twenty-eight years old and nine months pregnant with my second child. Yes, I chose to go on this rodeo again. Despite the stress, pain, mental breakdowns, lethargy, and more, at the end of the day, for me, it's all worth it. For anyone reading this book, I want you to take the time to reflect on the postpartum period. The postpartum period is not discussed often, and no one truly prepares a mother for that experience. Everyone is amped up and can give you books of information on being pregnant, being in labor, and giving birth, but where are the discussions on postpartum care?

Did you know that women get one postpartum checkup after giving birth at the six-week mark? Nothing else. You carry life inside you that transforms you physically, mentally, and spiritually for approximately nine months and only get one doctor's visit to check on you after the main event. It is simply not fair. It simply isn't enough. The scarcity of good available therapist is becoming harder and harder, yet our mental health persists. There are mothers without good support systems trying to do the best they can day by day. This book is meant to spark conversation and allow mothers to be honest with themselves. Let's not tippy-toe around difficult conversations. Let's just have them. With the lack of resources and minimal support, it's best for a community to openly talk about it and share our experiences so that every women knows they are not alone. Yeah, every experience is different, but it does not have to be a lonely one.

About the Author

Joclyn M. Polhemus was born and raised in Richmond, Virginia. Faith and family are the most important to her. As a mother of two, Joclyn saw the need to facilitate the conversation, which gave her the idea of her first book *42 Days Postpartum: A New Mom's Candid Memories.*